Ankylosaurs

Plated Dinosaurs

by Grace Hansen

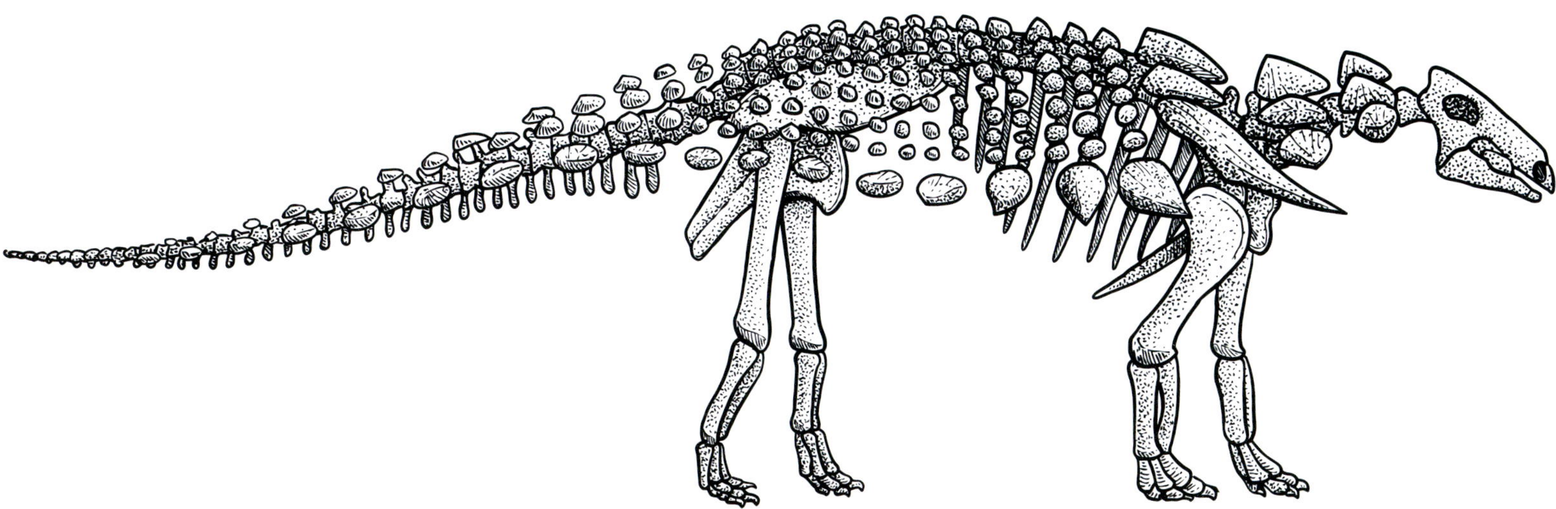

Abdo Kids Jumbo is an Imprint of Abdo Kids
abdobooks.com

abdobooks.com

Published by Abdo Kids, a division of ABDO, P.O. Box 398166, Minneapolis, Minnesota 55439.

Abdo Kids Jumbo™ is a trademark and logo of Abdo Kids.

Printed in the United States of America, North Mankato, Minnesota.

052025

092025

Photo Credits: Getty Images, Science Source, Shutterstock, ©London looks p.17/CC-BY-2.0

Production Contributors: Teddy Borth, Jennie Forsberg, Grace Hansen
Design Contributors: Candice Keimig, Pakou Moua

Library of Congress Control Number: 2024947620

Publisher's Cataloging-in-Publication Data

Names: Hansen, Grace, author.

Title: Ankylosaurs: plated dinosaurs / by Grace Hansen

Other Title: plated dinosaurs

Description: Minneapolis, Minnesota : Abdo Kids, 2026 | Series: Dinosaur groups | Includes online resources and index.

Identifiers: ISBN 9798384905141 (lib. bdg.) | ISBN 9798384905844 (ebook) | ISBN 9798384906193 (read-to-me ebook)

Subjects: LCSH: Dinosaurs--Juvenile literature. | Prehistoric animals--Juvenile literature. | Animals, Fossil--Juvenile literature. | Paleontology--Juvenile literature.

Classification: DDC 567.90--dc23

Table of Contents

The Plated Dinosaurs 4

Gastonia 14

Minmi 16

Talarurus 18

Ankylosaurus 20

Common Ankylosaur Features 22

Glossary 23

Index 24

Abdo Kids Code. 24

The Plated Dinosaurs

Ankylosaurs were a group of dinosaurs. They lived from the Middle Jurassic to the Late Cretaceous. They were found throughout the world.

Jurassic

201 million years ago

Cretaceous

145 million years ago

Ankylosaurs

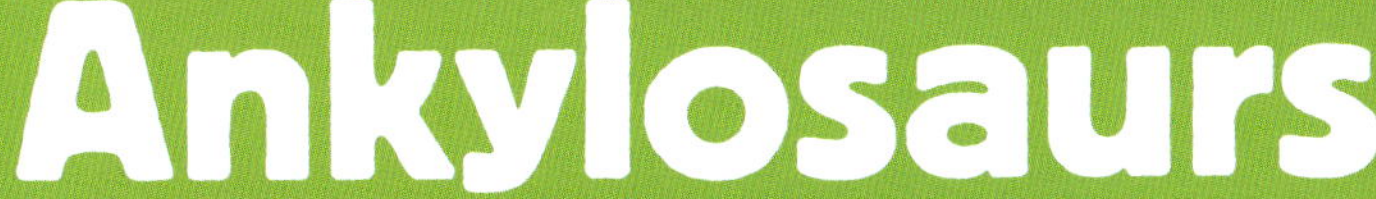

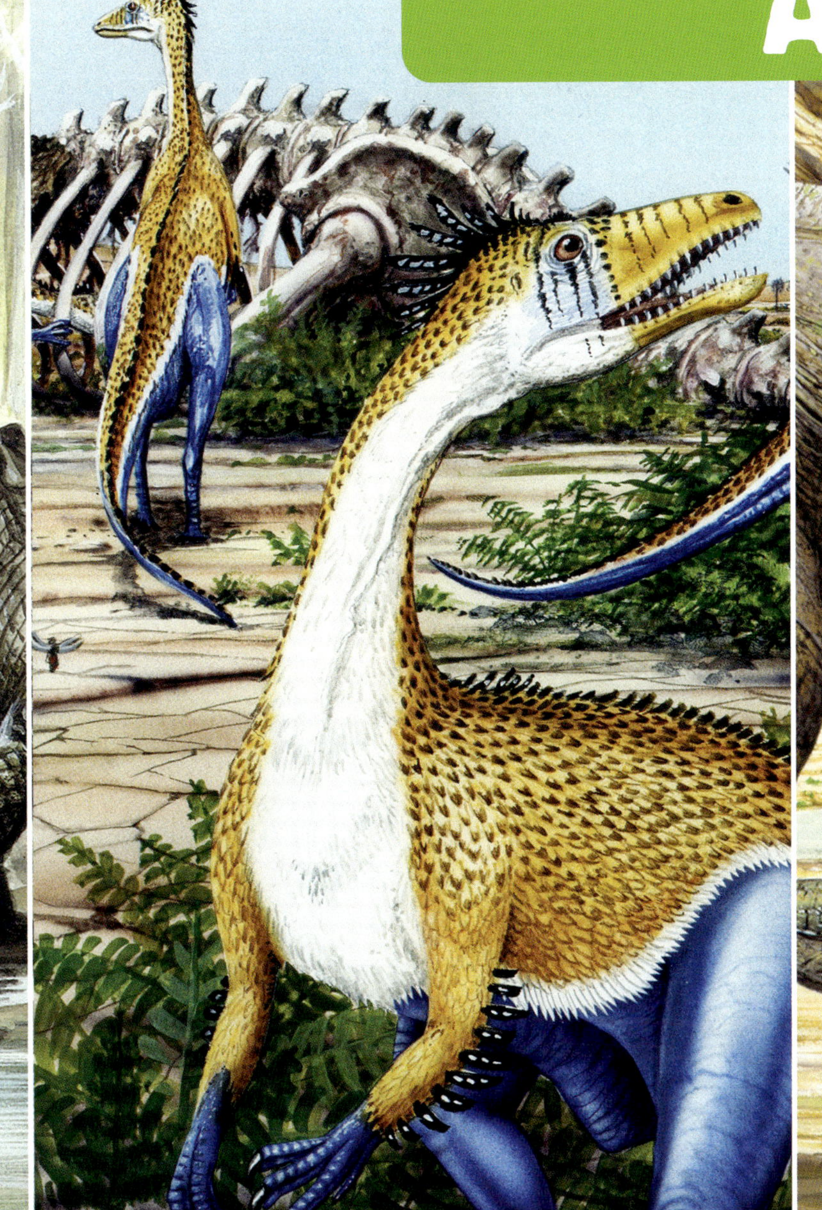

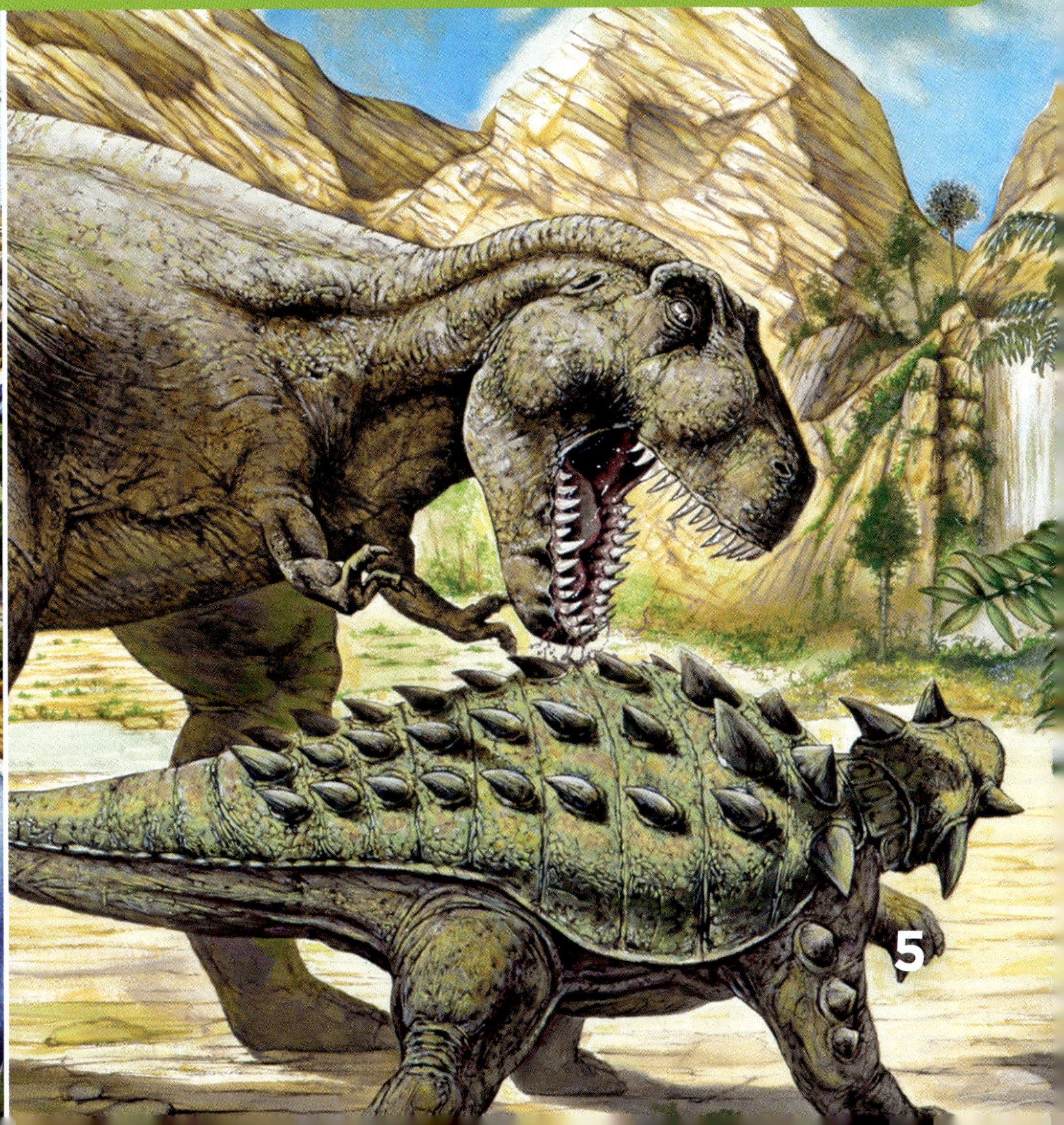

Ankylosaurs ranged in size. The smallest were about 5 feet (1.5 m) long. The largest could grow up to 30 feet (9 m)!

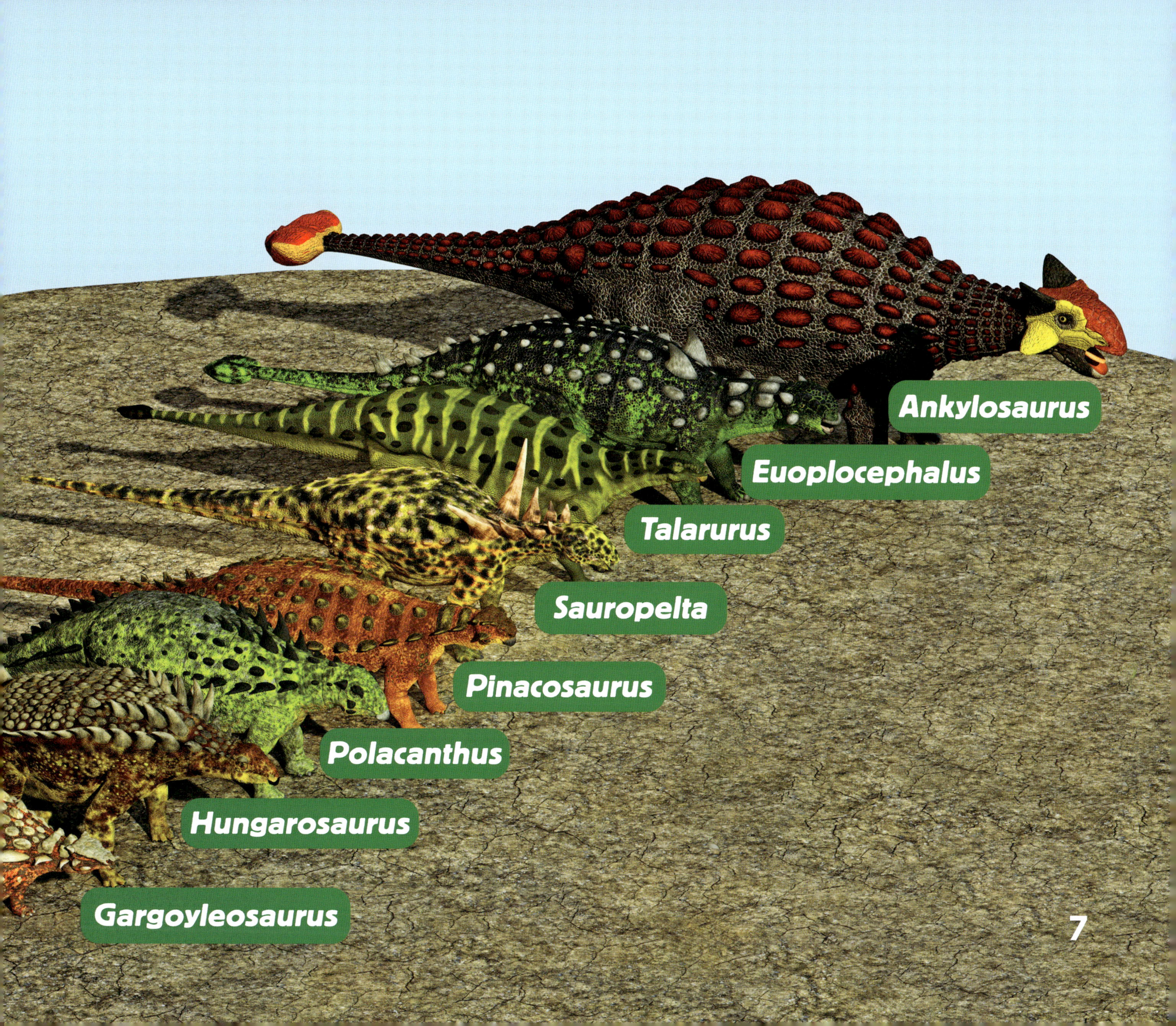
Ankylosaurus
Euoplocephalus
Talarurus
Sauropelta
Pinacosaurus
Polacanthus
Hungarosaurus
Gargoyleosaurus

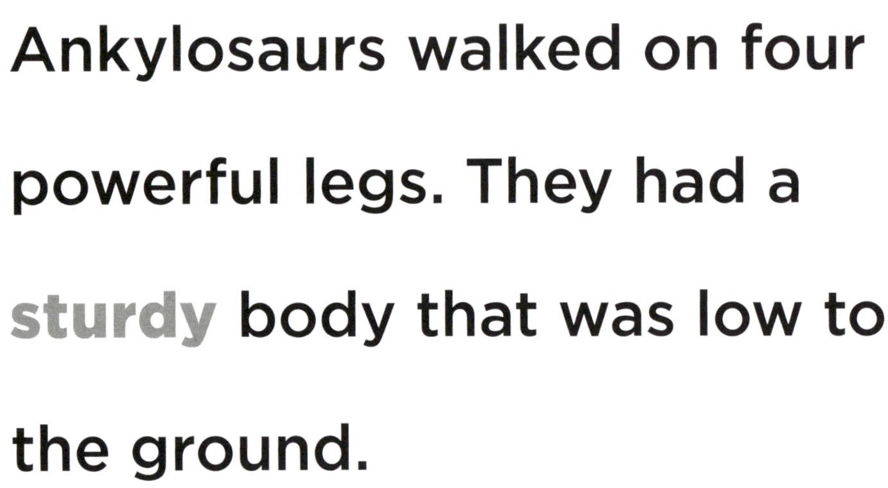

Ankylosaurs walked on four powerful legs. They had a **sturdy** body that was low to the ground.

Ankylosaurs had protective plates that covered most of their body. Some members of the group had a spiked tail or tail club. These kinds of tails were likely used for **defense**.

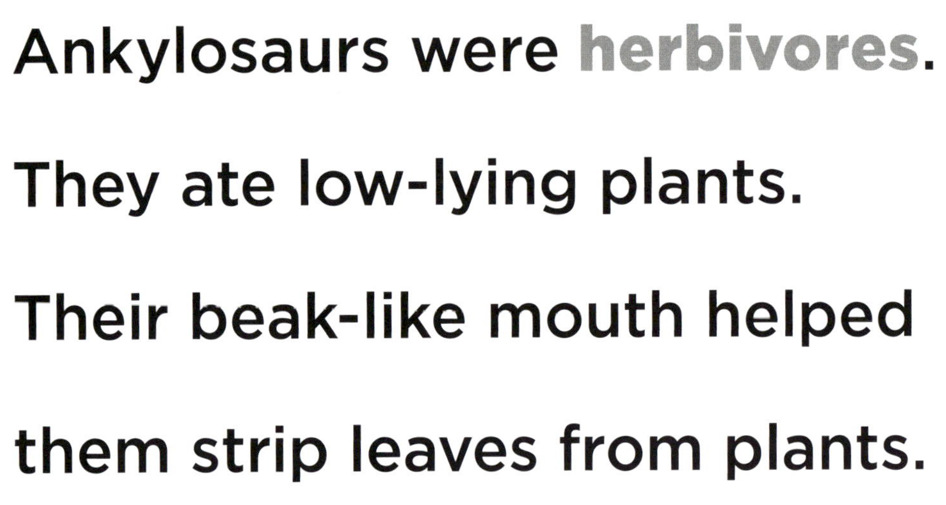

Ankylosaurs were **herbivores**.

They ate low-lying plants.

Their beak-like mouth helped

them strip leaves from plants.

Gastonia

Gastonia was a medium-sized ankylosaur. It had large shoulder spikes. It lived near forests and rivers.

Early Cretaceous
Fossils found in
North America
As long as a
canoe
16 ft (5 m) long
As heavy as a
white rhino
4,200 lbs
(1,905 kg)
Gastonia

Minmi

Minmi was a small ankylosaur. It had longer **limbs** than other dinosaurs of its kind. This helped *Minmi* run from **predators**.

Early Cretaceous
Fossils found in
Australia
As long as an
alligator
10 ft (3 m) long
As heavy as a
large motorcycle
660 lbs
(300 kg)
Minmi

Talarurus

Talarurus is one of the most well-known ankylosaurs. Many of its **fossils** have been discovered. Its name means "basket tail" or "wicker tail." This is because of its **unique** tail bones and club.

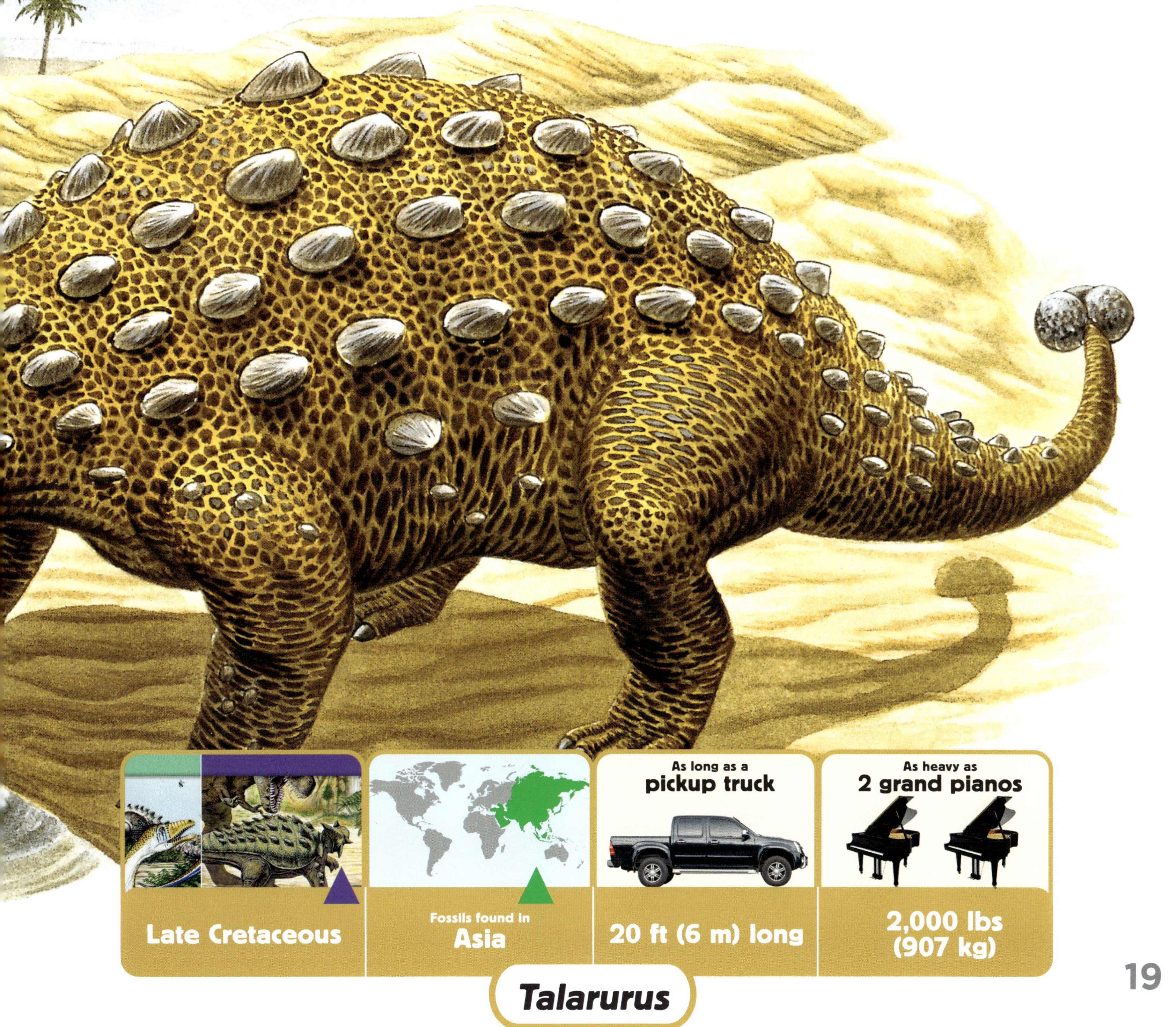

Late Cretaceous	Fossils found in Asia	20 ft (6 m) long	2,000 lbs (907 kg)

Talarurus

Ankylosaurus

Ankylosaurus is the most famous member of the group. It is also the largest-known ankylosaur. It had a heavy club on the end of its tail.

Late Cretaceous
Fossils found in
North America
As long as a
school bus
30 ft (9 m) long
As heavy as an
Asian Elephant
10,000 lbs
(4,536 kg)
Ankylosaurus

Common Ankylosaur Features

Glossary

defense – the act of protecting or guarding.

fossil – the remains or trace of a living animal or plant from a long time ago.

herbivore – an animal that only feeds on plants.

limb – a part of the body that can move and bend. Arms, legs, and wings are limbs.

predator – an animal that hunts other animals for food.

sturdy – strong or solid.

unique – being the only one of its type.

Index

body 8, 10

food 12

fossils 18

habitat 14

limbs 8, 16

mouth 12

movement 8, 16

plates 10

size 6, 14, 16, 20

spikes 14

tail 10, 18, 20

Visit **abdokids.com** to access crafts, games, videos, and more!